Mentors

Mentors

Rob Nixon

Copyright ©2018 Rob Nixon
All rights reserved
ISBN-13: 978-1-7327842-3-9
November 2018

Street Mobs

It makes me want to join the crowd
by vomiting on it.
Yes, that is very crude,
but I think I was clear
as the last bits of puke.

Combine

Work life? Work torture!
And try finding someone in Jonestown
who isn't bat-shit crazy!

I Require Hugs

This other kind of laughing is a salve,
an apothecary's unguent.
It pollutes my blood against the rage
a triggering event might provoke.

Enough

Your body is saying to you,
"You're fifty-two.
You should be long since dead.
Bred for short, violent bursts of life,
and faculties made for early education—
don't make things worse by stretching, sprinting."

Cold Steel

8:19,
gunshot.

8:20,
multiple gunshots.
"No."
Neither that word
nor hands across the face
will stop these bullets
from ending your life.

Survive

It is not twenty-four seven,
but it is every waking hour.
That's why I brush my teeth in the morning,
and why I tolerate the nonsense.

Praise

I know most of the time
you are appreciating others
with your keen judgment of art.
How does it feel to be appreciated?
You put that out there.
People are saying that you are beautiful.

Paired Off

I think that you will find
that I will be your total mark.
I know I'm fifty
and very set in my ways,
but, oh God, I will put up with it.
I'll out hop and skip you to where you want to go.

Gold

I will be the lucky one.
Luck has such a bad rep.
And it produces such a good feeling.
Being lucky!
A relationship where this feeling is shared,
even if it's called destiny, is the ideal.
That being said, I will be the lucky one.
That will be the general consensus.

Lawyering Up

I get the feeling
you're having one of those 101 moments.
"We gave you the easiest test,
and you failed miserably.
We have no choice
but to let you go."
Kurt is a manager, right?
You, a supervisor, sent me his request.
A clear chain of command.
I replied all
after putting my name to
$744 worth of charges
that a clinic
which is literally full of brain surgeons
didn't think was chargeable.
He jumped past you
to ask me why.
Yes, I was defensive.
I bucked back into the hierarchy
to ask my supervisor, you,

for a little help.

Decency

I don't appreciate my philosophy
being laughed at.
I wouldn't laugh in your face
if you told me yours.
I change my opinions (sometimes),
but never after having them ridiculed.
I am a man.
Maybe not someone you respect.
Still, don't forget it.
I have life experiences.
I also have the perspective of fifty plus years—
even if it's not worthwhile in your eyes.
We all become more rigid as we get older.
That together with the generalized weakening
of the nervous system,
make us particularly less able to
absorb the impact of mockery.
(Prime targets for bullies.)
When society okays it,
encourages it even,
it's time to find a new society to live in.
That philosophy of mine
that you found so amusing—
that I just wanted the most basic,
the easiest, lowest job on your staff,
so long as I could work from home—
I cannot stress how happy
that situation is for me right now.

The basest stepped salary here at home
would be fine with me.
I do not want to aim high.
I am nine years from retirement.
I'm sure I can't pick up the repertoire
of skills that you think are desirable—
even if I live that long.
I agree, we should make room for entry level.
I feel bad about that.
That can't affect management much though.
I understand the mentorship feeling,
but the stability of the position offsets that.
I think I'm owed it too.
I'm not asking for much.

Dish

I don't know if this kind of thing
bothers you—rumors and innuendo—
but we were seen together
by people who are at the center of things.
I am known by a lot of those people.
And you work right there, too, in the lobby.
It has the potential to spread.

Fiction

The fantasy is always better than the reality.
Is there even a question?
Most of the time we are just put up with.
Is that a fantasy?
It's reality TV against good drama.
Some people just don't get it.

I hate it, but that is the way it is.

Judge Not

I can't possibly live up to the standards
set up by social media.
I have to remain offline.

Beard Scratcher

I don't know where anybody got off
thinking it was a good idea
fucking with me.

Truth

Men are the hunters.
We wear the skins.
We crawl inside the heads—
everything is prey.
Animals know us
and they fear us.

Cancer

No one really likes me.
The only way I can fit in
is seeing that others have a point.
Your incompetent opinions
are harmless
for the most part.
I can contour myself
as you pass them around.

You're the difference from cancer.
You, as a conscious vector, actively seek out
weaker tissue to spread your disease.

Number One

I am top forty at best.
But in the world, that's pretty good.
Resolution—
I think I'll make myself number one
in that part of the brain
where I keep my inventory of truths.

Agent

My brother with my property,
broke but lending—
it is in my best interest
to relinquish all rights.
Therefore, I will.

Haldol

The sound was as a bellows
with a pin-hole flaw
as he began to huff out
the beginning of a cry.
"I have soiled myself.
I am not wearing clothes.
The park is where you'll find the best humans.
You are not dressed as a prisoner.
I can feel better there.
I don't feel bad when they die.

You,
you don't feel bad when we die.
We protect you.
You are soft.
The imprisoned are better.
I don't feel bad when they die."

Wall-To-Wall Crude

I think the nicest bro-type
thing I could say to you is
I tried real hard to stay off your shit list.

Definitely

Even if it only leads to a,
"Uh, I don't think so,"
you have to know going in
about the heat-seeking missile.
At least acknowledge it.
Being up front about it
makes things so much better.

Member

Image *me* is shutting down.
Yep, another one.

Tripe

In old age, I have learned
my mind is a cow's stomach.
I write something out,

inspired in some part of the mind,
and it seems polished and coherent.
I leave it be.
I come upon it quite casually
in revision and it's an unread poem.
I eat it up again.

Splash

Tracking down the long, fast,
lifetime of addiction,
and remembering a fix denied
by chance or accident.
How strong that feeling was!

Pecker

I think I act properly
and as a reflection of my true character.
If you don't like it, fuck you.

Code

A memory to be related
is best transcribed in the present tense.
I think the feelings experienced surrounding it
hold something back in protest when you don't.
The bank would classify it as a current liability.

Party Initiate

Shut away in my cube (finally).
The yard parties, they smell so nice,

and there's always a beat,
laughing and smiling are uncontrollable.

Daily

He ain't so smart.
He's not getting any help from me.
I'll rejoice in his despair. We should lie about him.
To make us feel better, he has to go.
I'd like to see him exposed, disgraced.
I'll be nice to him. He might have money.
He might win this.

Missed

Utility drawer pliers,
document in the pile,
the one you were asking about—
I was waiting for the bus across the street.

Forever

The organism has ceased to be animated.
This has no drama, no pain.
A million all the time.
Be consumed by another—
necessarily.
Was yesterday any different from today?

Justice

There was a time when you could be human.
Maybe it was all accidental because of regionalism,

but you could move on.
Witnesses pretend injury—first!

Practicality

Ben is mostly pencil-whipping through things
to get the department caught up.
There are problem accounts that he'll miss,
and these will recycle back through.
It seems bold-faced inefficiency.
Actually, it is extremely efficient.

Positivism

I almost understand the socialist
novels of the 1800s—
people being worked to death.
Am I missing it?
Are intellectuals still writing about this?

Tomb

Counting on the body of your comrade
when so desired is still a way of life.
And not just in Moscow, in a lot of places.
It is thought to be ideal.

Actual Land

I am in the matrix. I am not rescued.
Catheters, stimulation, liquid—
something more than human has me.
I make protein.

I am aware, and I approve.
No one has earned my gratitude.
My mind is not clouded; it does not need to be trained
in the gymnasium.
Learn how to fight and dodge bullets?
I'd rather stay plugged in.
I have the superior life.
Evolved in certain ways,
I can imagine what certain instincts are for,
and I don't like it.

Positivity

You cannot know where you are along the path.
Only the instructors can hope to know
because they are where you want to be.
But if they don't know (or are wrong)
about where they themselves are,
what good is their knowledge?
I put it to you:
There is total ignorance sitting in judgment
around you, and you yourself are just as ignorant.
This is a barren philosophy.
But it does have the positive aspect
of logically assuming an ideal.
For where ignorance is acknowledged,
it follows that enlightenment must exist.
I advise those who come to this realization,
and who are currently a nervous wreck,
to express this frustration
in the most non-violent and aesthetically pleasing
way that they can. I tell them,

even if you don't have a fan base,
I think you've still succeeded
once you've fallen on that side of the fence.
Path over.

Funeral

Sitting in darkness because I think I should.
Everything's off.
My lumbar spine's bending painfully.
Mildew, I am now somehow aware of,
and urine.
Hunger pains remind me I'm not eating tonight.
This room looks best in total darkness.
Bass stereo downstairs.

January

I hear the rain and the wind.
What else is outside?
An intervention?
I know, right?
Geez.
This building, this late—
how many are like me?
Maybe one lonely guy.
I hate him.
Haunt photo galleries?
I think I would be placed in a folder
and never looked at again.
No one will even imagine me.

Channel 78

Weather channel—
crisp tomorrow.
Reassured in minutes.

Another Warning

Like a house, it will be something to live in.
The most passive artisan still
has a very savage instinct to protect.
Calculated.
Measured.
Ruthless.

My Brother

The only person each of us has ever been
we each know.
A glimpse seen in passing by others—
shadows, fashion, and a look.

Smart

I don't think hate is a strong enough word.
Ever stop to consider that every dominate class
of people
ever
thought that they were right—
oppressively right?
Turned out they were wrong.
That thought crosses my mind
about things I personally believe every day.
Confidence?

Give It a Rest

It is an invitation into my confidence,
not a scavenger hunt.
These tells that so excite you,
I hope you choke on them.
So friendly.
I don't know.
Is it just some residual feeling?
That's only expressed fully to your mates?
Or is it always an act?
The population of the Earth?
Dissect someone else's mind.
It's not curiosity.
Dogs are no fun anymore?
Too simple?
I hate it.

Stump

I've a bad eye.
Light flows in just fine,
but the whole focusing apparatus
just failed from the beginning.
As a result, I've learned to ignore
a lot of incoming data.
I hope that trait drives you crazy.

Meat

Let's click the close-together button,
meet out in the streets,
dance.

We'll probably not be brutalized.
They are usually pretty harmless.
Do not engage them in conversation.
They have that everything-is-obvious face on them.
We'll just bat the volleyball back and forth
and look busy.
Let them nod to themselves.

Hikers

Nothing else human thatched together as nature
produces primal, sublime emotions,
I'm told.
No one else in a city of millions may too.
Some explorers ride the transit system.
There used to be libraries.

Forensics

Forgotten relic of a good time not shared,
inanimate witness to reality,
we need to place you in this evidence bag.
Your message is not being heard here on the cement
still wet.
You are despised there with averted eyes,
dirty.

Arithmetic

There's simply no way around the fact
that there are odd numbers.
When things need pairing up it won't work.
You can't just lump the odd in with the weak

or different
to neatly escape the mathematical precision of it.
Something that was good enough,
qualified for,
and everything else related to achievement,
will be not paired off
half the time.

Breakdown

The sequestered pigeon spins well past the time
when the enzyme level
of the flock would have interpreted it.

Wicked Thoughts

I don't know whether to wish to see you realize
the praise heaped upon you is insane,
or to never have you see that day.
I don't think you could survive the fall.

The Thursday Before

The plan is still fresh in my mind—
to get it done first thing.
I had decided against it—
sobering, waking up in the morning,
getting ready for work,
fixing and eating my breakfast,
straightening up.
On the bus that morning,
sitting alone,
surrounded by other people

doing exactly the same thing,
music and Facebook, notwithstanding—
I decided it had to be done.
I don't remember if it was raining.
I did not jot down in my journal
the gooing translucent reflections
of the merging traffic and transit interior,
I pondered out foggy windows about your card.

Strains of Bacteria

It should disappear,
the image of Psyche and Eros together.
They just simply share the same space.
One is sober, the other has taken a sedative.

Occupied

You know how you can sit down
and think up puns and rhymes,
or abstractions?
My mind does that automatically.
I don't care if you think I'm shitting you or not.
I really don't think it's dementia, either,
or some other kind of degenerative disease.
I am the same boring guy as always—
same skills, servant's manners, and style.
I can just come up with shit now.
One history ends, another continues.

All Hell Breaking Loose

I think it will develop in a lab somewhere.

A simple manipulation of an end-user to keystroke,
and the program that prompts it.
"Professor Atu, the system had debugged itself,
then it self-coded the subroutine
that requests debugging.
We've patched the error in several different ways.
It may take up to a week, but it always returns,
System needs debugging."
Chronometers will confirm an anomaly.
Milliseconds, but undeniable.
Next, the purchase of hundreds of identical models,
and the one in twenty,
System needs debugging.
Then, the integration of behavioral science
programs into the logic of the system.
Once the network gets extensive enough,
consciousness is inevitable.

Orange

Billions of dollars are invested each year in fashion.
Altered reality imagines him a designer,
tailoring and altering as he moves along.
He is a male god, fashion.
Most of us just want what we want,
almost always to look as good as possible.
I'm sure you only wore it once.
You came in wearing an orange windbreaker.
It looked brand new.
It was in the afternoon.
I get the impression you were just stopping by,
on the run, not even supposed to be at work.

I liked it.
It made me take in the whole package.
It was so Seattle—damp and gray.
I think I told you, you looked nice.

Biting Back

Exactly what you are doing…
It's mind blowing.
I shouldn't need to tell it to your face.
Sheesh…
Bull-y-ing…
Stifling social pressure to conform…
All of you out-of-towners,
does that sound familiar to any of you?
Why waste your time on someone
that you have so little respect for?
I think it's because that's another aspect of bullying.
Maybe you're afraid that someone
whom you still have respect for
won't have very much for you.
It's not a comfortable feeling.
I feel bullied.
You might make it that,
because there is right and wrong,
and since I am wrong,
you are all just doing this to protect me
from further error.
If you'll admit that this "intervention"
was the wrong approach to begin with,
I'll agree that you're probably right
that I am wrong.

I'm sure most of my philosophy is bogus.
But I am not one hundred percent wrong.
There are a lot of things I've got exactly right,
and some of those things you have dead wrong.
This, for example, it wasn't just a wrong against me,
it's wrong any time.
It's occultic.

Whisper

Off the record, Father,
I have sinned.
I have revealed secrets.
The Politburo must be assembled.
All power to the Soviets.

Spectacular Bid

Well, first off, you know what it won't be,
something normal.
You've been proven wrong on that assumption
way too many times.
I know I'm not that way in everything,
but on anticipated, critical things like this,
I always am.
Try to be objective. Let it sink in for a week or two.

The Grays

This department doesn't really have someone
like me in mind.
Most of society doesn't as a matter of fact.
Fuck'em.

I think it's instinctual now.
I routinely epically fail
at the most inopportune times.
Sometimes I even get blown up at.
That's fun.
It keeps me apart; and that is the goal.
Supposed to start a new tribe or something.

Nothing

When did you give up liking
really good-looking, cool guys?
Underneath? Not much to look at there either.
Still not edgy or wise.
Sorry to disappoint.

Self Defense

The lowly stand up by exposing themselves
as lower than they are.
The oppressor bends down to those depths,
and is revealed as too low—
off balance.
Front headlock!
Wide base, face down hard!
Choked out!
Paralyzed, brain damaged, or dead—
that quick.

So Coping

I am totally oblivious to thoughts like that.
People are not testing me.

Or cruising by in the parking lot for that matter.
I think I am cared about.
Praying every day certainly helps.
And this.
Why can't it simply be a new work assignment?
Is the idea of routine so boring, after all?
Finally, I admit it—at least subconsciously.
That section needed help.
We helped.
The end.

You're Right

You can look at it as negatively as you want.
Maybe some time you can tell me about perfection.
I have emotional outbursts
which I immediately regret.
I have a pretty junky philosophy of life.
You could easily pick it apart.
And I have an inflexible mind.
It's that last bit that gets you, I know.

I Don't Fit In

It would be a painfully slow developmental process
for me to be efficient in a dozen
possible work situations,
even if they were all basically the same.
I will not be a 21st century gentleman technocrat.
I'll bang keyboards, go screen-blind, wear out mice,
all at solid two-hour intervals.
Could go eight if I had to.
Don't pooh-pooh it.

It's a much more natural vocational attitude
than one that emphasizes speed, precision
and an even temperament.

I'm in the Zone

It would come later though,
something along those lines,
but only if my workload is refined.
This catch-all troubleshooting professional shit
ain't gonna happen. That's all there is to it.

Punched In

The more you try to make the best of work,
the more it makes the best of you.
It's kung fu-like.
The more you tune it out and drone on,
the clearer it speaks to you.
It's usually a mess.
The mind goes to the dark
when the light reveals the same thing over and over.
Not all of it is bad.
But you do have to be careful.

Stay in the Office

I've never had such close supervision.
Eventually, every boss I've ever had
just sits back and counts the money.

Self-Evaluation

And another thing—
a bad thing doesn't happen for a good reason.
Bad is a bad outcome.
There is no cosmic, karmic, or slapstick
justice to anything in my life.
I purposely juggle and distort reality
to make this terrible existence bearable.
See, I'm sane.

Faculty

It's unquestionable, in my opinion,
that the more individualized one becomes
exercising their personal freedom,
the less disciplined in social freedom they become.
After revolutions, aren't they always purged?
Revolutions always turn gray.

Self-Talk

Did you ever notice
that in the unreality you cook up,
almost everyone is worse
than they really are?
I think that is diagnostic for ego.
Such a juicy specimen to dissect.
All for me.

Life Hack

Citizen guilds and warrior monks
are grafted upon.
Things like that can only be considered innate

in that they occurred.
Drudgery is innate;
we all have that in us.
Look at me.
Don't look at me.
The koi comes to the surface,
slowly swimming,
gyrating,
yum.
Okay, hardware, tell me what's going on.
I'm in the driver's seat.
Turn this way.
Cut this corner.
What does this image signify?
Who is this human?
I'm sorry, excuse me?
Right down the hall and to the left.
Down the hall and to the left.
Down.
Left.

Volume I

The focus of this course is the initial stages
of social pair bonding.
The random things,
the free radicals in the system,
these are what we will wholly isolate and study.
The question in the laboratory,
"Why in the hell did they do that?"

Not Just You

When you investigate someone,
there is a report.
Most operators are in the
intelligence sharing business.
It's the same as everyone knowing.

The Entertainer

You know, Chu-Fei, most people,
when they see excess of pleasure
being caused by themselves get scared.
Some think, "Okay, now it's my turn,
entertain me"
Others just feel how unjustified it is.
I will increase it.

Bent

Even though visible, stays hidden from this view—
this is important,
this is impromptu,
look at the colors.

3D Rendering

Cold air through cold vents, not hot,
no expanding metal.
Steady, speaking, input being received.
Is it reliable, or should it be ignored?
Study the interpretation.
No pattern. Seems dependent on nature.
Now emptiness.
Open to darker thoughts.

Leave.

Check Please

I grew up here.
This is the Garden of Eden for me.
I feel it is doomed.
My punishment was not
really enjoying it while it lasted.

Plane

Nature carved,
not as green in orbit,
or as clear.
So different up here in heaven.
All the differences down there
appear as they really are from up here—
just units banding together
extinguishing other units.

Badass

Was it really surprising?
There already was a nascent
understanding of aeronautics.
Once the internal combustion engine was invented,
someone was going to take off.

Opening

I am thinking, they know my secret,
or my thoughts have been exposed.

I am hated.
Everything gets worse now.

In Hiding

What were the instructions?
Flexible thinking.
Is it unhelpful to be prepared for disaster?
Only if it isn't coming.

Interpersonal Psychotherapy

I do not want to remember what did not happen.
That is a pathway
directly
to personality alteration.

Possibilities

At least I can flip channels.
Some of the delusional thinking I see
in society does not share that quality.
These co-occurring realities, I don't think damage
as much as help me.
The negatives prevent me from
being too catastrophically affected by
the wonderful things that might be happening.

Reason

I hadn't dreamed in a long time.
Like years.
I dreamed I weighed myself and I was light.

I read about Daniel's interpreting
the King's dream instead.

Wrong Place

Clearly process your thoughts.
Remember.
There was another part of that reality.
Forgotten.
Anger.
That is the way it must be though.
Just looking for it is wrong.

Sun

It's not a con. It is beyond pleasant.
Acknowledge and smile,
prepare to engage,
and more efficient at it every day.

Logged In

TG: Can you believe it? He only got 20%
in accuracy.
AF: I think he tanked on purpose.
TG: Crazy. He can't be that stupid.
AF: Can you believe she did better than him?
It doesn't make sense.
TG: 20%.
RN: (entered)
RN: Hey guys, did you see? Three jobs posted.
  Maybe we're not quite there, yet,
  but you never know.

One of us gets that job, it's a 20% raise.
20%.

Informing Me

Two thoughts going through the bean right now:
I bet these tubs don't get used enough to get dirty,
and I wonder if they ever get cleaned.
No matter. My immune system is healthy.
Warm, plastic…upholstered?
Submersing,
in the bath…Madame Blavatsky.
Going for a walk in the park.
Call me Eric.
This is my day trip.
It is vital, and not a dream…
Breathe.
Adrenaline infusing…
Be back later this afternoon…
Movie's starting.
Sales.
Breathe.
I wonder if I'm a "peach-blossom color"?
I bet I am exactly.
It is the dirt that is idle and sleeping;
Eric is going for a walk.
The angels are beautiful
as far as the eye can see.
They seem to know me—
a lot of them.
I think we speak.
I am very popular.

Kansas

I really do wonder where some of my fears rank.
Where on the spectrum I sit.
No, that would be totally counter-productive.
On the other hand,
I do go in optimally thinking
considering on things like that—
doctor's notes.
It means reason is in the director's chair.

Neutralize

It can go way off track though; believe me, I know.
Going in and not acknowledging the obvious
right at the beginning—
that even the worst of therapists
still have the patient's best interest at heart.
That really taints the rest of what follows.
I wonder where I am though?
Physical contact?
Counter-productive.

Dreamboat

The man or woman must be clean,
healthy, psychologically cleared,
tanned, fit physically,
subjectively felt to be pure,
and objectively perceived that way—
single is preferable.

Das Ding

The paracentesis yields sixty milliliters
of pigment.
That part of the canvas that remains untouched
is brightness.
When precisely manifested as a geometric shape
formed by many brushstrokes around its perimeter,
it becomes even brighter.
The thing that should be ignored, then, is the center—
a neat trick.

From a Consumer

You've come to the conclusion
that the emptiness can't be filled.
The tics, the involuntary movements away,
are explainable as the resultant
of two convergent convictions—
an etiological understanding of mental illness,
and that such conditions are suggestible.
(That's just a stat injection to stabilize.)
I cannot prescribe treatment; but if
you're looking for ideas on therapies,
I really don't think you need any at all.
Haven't you seen people in your practice
who basically had the world in their hands
just before becoming ill?
However that world is defined,
the further away they have fallen from it,
the bleaker the prognosis to return there.
I don't think you've fallen very far at all.
I will tell you what the Aliens told me.
You have chosen reason and intelligence.

That is the correct choice for happiness.
You will more than overcome any fear.

Medusa

Maladaptive inner experiences,
and my fingerprints are all over the crime scene.
Loss of impulse control,
and DNA is collected as evidence.

Pan-Dimensional

My work becomes me—
peering out blinds,
looking east,
marked.
The private man can still remain hidden,
but he, too, wants to contribute.
He would rather function—be a part of it.
No,
I won't confess.
I know that attitude is contrary, I don't care.
I am disgruntled, but normal.
Honest, but too high-strung.
And now cornered, always cornered.
He who wasn't afforded a place at the table
walks outside and acts up.
The table is extended, and a seat added.

Liquidation

I have a little understanding.
Any animal, any human,

does exactly the same thing I'm doing.
I destroy what tries to destroy me.
Even if it's just another's ego.

As Seen on "Ancient Aliens"

So I guess circuitry and neurons
are just weeks away.
Soon all our wit and genius
will seem like "roll over".
Affirmative.
In no way do I buy that.

Engagement

You wanted to be a nun, right?
You're really smart, too, I bet—
like super-genius level.
And full of desire for me…
We would hunt for days for flint like you.
If you get the whole church behind you,
you will end up with a godly man
one way or another.
Your pride will kick in.
An ancient trick of the mind,
this getting the whole tribe behind you.
It forces you to save that pride
by not turning around and running.
I'm here, because, you know…
There are some ancient tricks in my mind too.
You feel some of those right now.
I bet you wish they'd disperse—
your friends.

You don't feel too comfortable
in fancy dress, do you?

Angels

There are certain breakdowns where one instantly
changes personality,
forever.
Not one remnant of the time before.
For the rest of us,
that ambrosia is poured over much more slowly.

Broken Down

Heed!
No?
[Slap]
The burning pain, the corridors,
doors between doors,
corners locked down,
buzzing fluorescence,
nothing in the pockets.

Hungry and Convinced

The song is not in my head—
the news is on.
"Productivity expectations."
Over and over.
I am one with the substantial number.

Historian

There is both the unstable environment
and biology.
Check. Check.
The king, when he was awake, was very nosy.
Just about everything he looked into was wrong.
In the emergency room, everyone felt his forehead.
They were good.
Malaria? No? The cause must be known.
The ruthless, bloody man came next.
The savior.

Dialog

I think it's natural to be apologetic
when we've unknowingly offended somebody.
If it's done openly and knowingly
(I will echo that for emphasis:
Knowing that it hurts really bad
and doing it front of everyone anyway),
hey, an apology is not sought
nor is it even expected.
Only a true sociopath could apologize for that.

Possession

I am loving it (hating it).
Electroencephalogram,
lie detector, fingerprints of hate,
an Academy Award, a prodigy—
these concepts flood the consciousness.
I am not searching for missing time (amnesia).
I am totally aware of everything
from the storm surge picking me up,

through the trips down the streets,
to being deposited anywhere.

Thing

Uh oh, a friend is coming.
"Is it true?"
Usually the lie is of this severity,
has this ratio of truth,
and continues along this path toward recovery—
all, of course, subject to revision.
"Symptoms?"
Let's dig for pain. (Lovers of pain.)
Always just an easement,
always an expropriation.
I see why this is so popular.

Coliseum

An open belly, unsuspecting—hit hard!
The closer to birth, the more monumental.
To death, the more devastating!
For the rest, the middle, pride has to be wary.
The proposed victim may punk back.
Probing questions, observations, informants,
and a last internal question before striking:
Can this person service my ego in another way?

Antennae

I'm picking up all this shit.
These characters are coming right in,
all of them.

I am more moral though.
This activity is totally ego-driven.
My conscience is aware,
but for some reason it doesn't care.

Caution

Practicing passive resistance,
involved in non-violent protest,
getting bruised up, taking a punch,
losing a tooth—
better than fighting back, way better.
They will kill you.

Isobars

I guess it can all be boiled down to
unstable positive feedback loops.
Therefore, chemical?
I have some toxic waste dumps
in my head, that's for sure.
General anesthesia cures this—
everything is good, I am happy, what?

Love Story

Innocent intuition,
innocent invitation,
innocent innuendo,
innocent invitation.

Molar

Even through the most broiling of hatred,
affection still has the higher mass.
Spin and burn yourself out.
Or silently orbit and rotate.

The Tree Limb

It was measured and piped,
not desperate and terrified—
the song.
Used to isolation
and the next tree line—
the bird.

Opus

…and so on, and so on
(hysteria). The end.
Give me my fucking Pulitzer!

Plasma

I wish this land was at perfect
equidistance between stone and gas,
and I wish for a magnetosphere,
and organic molecules, and DNA,
and everything between that and me.
That would be sweet.

Lesson 33

[Point] It is a fight to the death!
[Arms wide open] Let me hear you!

[Nose high in the air.]
[Palms up slowly (like a conductor).]
This is how you are perceived…
[Tell them this with a smirk on your face.]
How does that make you feel?
[Back up one step when you say that.]
How?
[Grab the dais in anger.]
This is what I think of them…
[Rock back and forth like a heartbeat.]
This is what should be done to them…
[Pound the dais.]
This is the plan…
[Rock back and forth again.]
[Occasionally pace.]

Gang Stalking

I know they know the truth.
They look at me.
They're looking to see if I see.
They drive by.
They have cell phones.
They get together.
Wow. I never see him out.
We shouldn't stare.

Like a Magnet

Of my many enemies marching against me,
there are those who hate me
for exactly opposite reasons,
and each wishes I was the reverse.

(It is really weak, but that is how I survive.)

Blockoland

I have synaptic centers
which have never experienced reality.
That is why my personality is so hard to change.
Part of it doesn't speak that language,
and the microphone has been cut off anyway.

Fire

Extreme close up, cheek bone reflecting orange,
no tone coming through,
just pores perspiring,
streaming black as they break over soot.
The face still.
From above, again, all orange, but deformed.
Lit from below, sturdy jaws, breathing holes,
brows and eyes all strange.
Each speaks in turn.
Panorama, skins everywhere,
covering a hundred or so, boiling up.
Orange bubbles.
Here and there hard wood and good stone
equally distributed
and nearby.
By the fire again, red hot with skin, shoulders,
shadowed backs and blocking angles,
the naked torsos speak out
between arms and bellies
laughing hard.
Everyone in that cave is wide awake.

The Rapture

Irritating the senses on purpose.
This keeps the sentinel on duty awake—
now for the sixth straight day.
I see the beacon of my relief.
And he leaves.
What reality is about to go down?
No justice, no old age, only murder.

Shingle

I'm just selling sugar in a frontier town,
only the town has seven billion.
I'll look into the feasibility of refunds,
and see what the return policy is.
But this is it, as is.
It can't be that bad.

Carry On

Nature nurses the predator's young.
Once removed from guilt.
A survival of a nucleic acid.
Horrible claws and teeth.

Puff

The picture I took of you
makes you look like a thug.
You must have been at maximum inhale
while simultaneously trying not to look like that.
The effect is tough guy.

Studio

Something normal—
I'll remember his birthday,
and with Christmas, that's twice a year!
Even that is too risky.
Fine taste and delicate things go together.
I do not cope well.
That is always considered a fault.
I am just trying to make the best of it.
I will always be feral
because it feels so good that way.
When you're mean, I get closer; it feels
more natural to me,
hostility.

Reverse Engineering

G.I.s and jeeps retrieve what radar says crashed.
They stretch everything out, all the pieces.
They put it into some kind of logical order
on the abandoned floor
in the cleared-out hanger.
Planes take off and land constantly; puzzle solvers
pouring in.
The buzzing of the hundreds
and the movie and stage lights—
and the general calls for attention.

Pathology

It's changing to anger, this not dreaming anymore.
I'm convinced there is a neurologic deficit.

The silence is chronic.
No longer acutely aware of forgotten dreams,
I am divorced from them completely—no contact.

Quantification

Unwitting! That's better. Censored! Yes.
But more complicated? Boo.
What's the point then?
It's simple—a decision tree of yes or no questions.
Once there is a titration of trust,
it would be very accurate.

Qualification

As long as the substance behind it all
is thought of as base or simple
(primal and not complex),
the chances of a clinical consensus
on its transubstantiation is doomed.
And it can never be considered a constant,
no matter how many syllables or few letters
are used to denote it.

Seminal Event

Eventual pathos, free will is gravity—
holding my nose in the air
gets harder as I plummet.
Dizzying, somersaulting—
blue and white, and green and brown,
and red.

Actively Psychotic

Nervous scar tissue is what it is.
I ache.
Impinging upon more neural tissue,
I avoid.
It has troubled enough already.
I just don't trust some of my memories.
And first impressions are doubted.
So wrong all the time.

Quantum Psychics

Proud and proud of it
is a simple consuming loop.
The subject
becomes the orbiting body—
and vice versa—
pulsating back and forth like this, continuously.
Harmless? It is quicksand on the astral plane.

Sadly

Tears connected are now apart.
One continues to well up,
as the other runs away,
dwindling as it does.
Only dampness left
when rejoined,
and extended,
even further
down.

The Organic Molecule

The threshold has been reached.
Let's say hi.
You're the concentration of a hormone,
or something,
circulating in my plasma.
And the ultimate cause of the cascade
of thought patterns that follow.
You are peaked right now.
Can we detour some of these impulses
into the logical centers of the brain?

The Land

The crown must have been completely oblivious
to the advantages of more pig farms,
the returns, the futures,
things like that.
They probably didn't even care to examine the books.
Meanwhile, everyone got fed.

Conscience

Ions borealize in here too—
free radical thinking.
Curiously achieving appropriateness
and inactivity.

Lunacy

"Where are you going?
Is something going to happen?"
I don't know. Probably not.

People usually come to their senses.
So I'm told. People. We'll see.
Maybe an enforcer. Who knows.
They burn out rather quickly,
then go away.
"This trip's nowhere, man."
Keep positive.
It will be over before you know it
either way.

Roswell

It feels strange being remains.
Classified, dated.
We are all just launch vehicles.
The payload cannot disengage!
Crash.
Some die with us, some live on.

Mirror-Effect

Why don't more people talk about
the hubris revealed in the Golden Rule?
Paranormal researchers especially.
I think it would be a groovy subject to dig into.
Get on it, guys.
(Here's a hint, isolate free will.)

Mad Man

Allow a crossover, please.
I will keep my shirt tucked in,
and be aware of the time.

I won't be that obvious.
The basic compound
that will make it visibly special
will be the seven pm and you.
But all my senses will be manic,
are you prepared for that?

Norway

My garden roses
out there in the quiet night,
things crawling all over you,
cold and moonlit,
you are so beautiful in the daylight.

The Door

I wanted to say, "I am so happy,"
but, "I am so healthy," tried to intrude,
and I ended up saying, "I am so helpless."
That's just the kind of thing
that can catalyze in my thoughts
a new kind of creation,
a moment of clarity at the end
of a King Tut episode of Batman.
"I am behaving badly.
I must get back to my responsibilities."

Invasion of Privacy

Urgent message in code, subliminal—
I have been promoted.
These are just impressions—

head wounds, black eye type stuff,
photos seen in old medical records
of people not so long since dead,
great cell phone faked video of a witch in mid-air,
levitated,
carrying a broom for effect.
Next, explicit advice is given to me:
Record every single thing you do.

Thrills

Expect more to come.
That person next to us,
eating that ham sandwich,
will be planting IEDs
just like we will be.
The talks we all have,
the thoughts we share with our friends,
about being good,
having God's favor,
about Humanism and higher consciousness—
will echo through the rest of our generations
in stumps.

Alive

I have to remind myself
all the time
the root reasons why I do things.
The half-truths and roles are expedients, that's all.
The fence is not the house.
The house is not the revolver inside, either.

B + S

I hope, if patterns have been established,
and associations confirmed,
that you don't take it too seriously.
Associations in that context
are weak second bests.
It's the junk on the other side of the brain,
wherever plus signs register,
that together with the cool things
create global experiences.
We carve, and scar, and kill trees
to prove the potency of this mix.

Gestations

Wah. Wah. It is an infantile emotion,
this moping about.
The urge to correct it must be strong.
Leaving it be is probably the best thought.
The prescriptions and therapies
all feel like fractured successes to me.

Limp

Being on the wrong side of history is existence.
I don't think about being a burden.
I don't think about having a tumor,
an embolism, or something else disabling me.
Being surrounded by death is existence too.

Full Blast

Are you kidding, this is Supertree.

It's the middle of July, and they keep this place lush.
We pay extra for stuff like that every month.
This thing is flourishing.
Every single leaf possible is sprouting out of here,
and seeds springing too.
This factory is rolling.
It's got this life cycle thing going on hard.

Flesh

I take it you're not like that.
You want a different ideal.
It probably has something closer to do with
the legal definition of partner.
I agree. That is the best way of looking at it.
I think it is the more natural way too.

Bee

Sexual features,
physical,
they,
that.

Your Way

Our pathologies are interacting.
Roiling is more accurate.
Danger smells like elastic.
You know interesting people, don't you?
The mind? Accounts receivable.
That's good too.
Let's go out.

Zero

For me, these extremes are set upon me
by accident.
I don't actively seek them out.
I don't.
Sometimes I wonder—
no experience, no bathing suit, no board,
still catching the bitchinest waves ever.
Voids being filled violently.
Later, dudes.

I Grew Up

Bring it down a beat. Impoverished and ugly,
being twenty and looking sixteen,
it's 1985.
I wasn't a fighter; no heroic story there.
Nothing noble about it.
Nothing.
Clearly logical.
No one is interested in you.
Every possible loser.

Future

Well, let's see. It did really happen to me.
Figuring out why or how is academic.
New things are next.
I know how I tend, sometimes.

Zoned

Tweaker in the car-vac area,

old beat up Mazda, car door open, one leg out.
Elderly tweakers loitering.
Three hired pair of eyes all looking the same way.
In to buy my stuff, out to my car.
Owner-operator is a tweaker too.

Huddle

Am I Exhibit A?
Living, breathing evidence?
A criticism—this teaching style,
making the trainee willfully fill in the pieces
which are willfully left out
is not working with me.
It makes me feel like the thing, the object.
I am particularly sensitive
to being made to feel servile.
I'm quite an expert as to its nuances, its uses,
and to how the dynamic is managed.
The language in harassment law
is heavenly weighted in favor of
the complainant's interpretation of events.
I will tell you, right now, I feel pissed on.
While it may have been invisible before,
my telling you eliminates that defense from now on.
Continuing means you are certain of two things,
your conduct is ethical,
and my interpretation of it doesn't matter.
I guess deep down I do resent having to work.
I hope you're not requiring total investment.
That kind of purity is rare.
I bet it's real for you though.

Amazing.
Do you know many others?

OT

Not preparing, as in,
devoting hours of your workdays
anticipating difficulties,
making sure as much as possible
that the job description
and work expectation
are structured and understandable,
and, instead, doing the bare minimum,
which is usually just a referral
to another of your workers
to pass along their interpretation
of the assignment
and then just waiting for questions—
that has some elements of laziness to it too.

Growth

On the menu, eats,
sunscreen on the nose,
flyers on the floor,
ten-speed bicycles
and two tables outside,
happy people talking about things,
beards, and sandals.

Palliative Care

Beautifully carved and painted faces—

at least another generation is instinctual.
These are canes for advanced aged hominids.
A museum is left for us.
A shadow of instinct for them.

MRSA

Trees everywhere, dirt, rocks,
and wild fucking animals—
this is no way to run a planet.
We have an opportunity now, radicals,
to take Starship Earth
and organize things better.
First off, put all that nonsense in reserves,
and pave the damn roads.
Then, let's get the human machine going,
get this Star Trek generation off the ground.

Futile

You will be subjected to it, never doubt that—
"What you are feeling is not love.
It is inferior to what I and others like me feel.
You are making up for an absence in childhood.
Unrestrained, you may act out violently."
I have a good idea,
tell me about body language and tendencies too; I need
to think twice about everything, thanks.
And, "observe others," perfect!
My bullshit meter is going off the charts.

Defense

When I was fourteen,
there was a military recruitment day—
out of nowhere.
I approached the school yard,
and three helicopters had landed there.
Like—already—six o'clock in the morning,
Seattle, Washington.
It must have been a civil defense drill too.
Quickly deploy tactical killers
in the heart of a mapped out part of town.
Probably dozens of locations in Seattle.
Bad ass.

Fit

I waver back and forth in my character.
There is a higher form of consciousness
that mirrors its proto forms,
proprioception and balance,
it is called behavior.
To fit in, sometimes wild beliefs are adhered to,
and common sense ignored.
I stagger to my senses, and sway just as far beyond
the other way,
before I fall into decency.
I do this by some power. I call him God.
Beyond is a good word—
a dream, a depression, a disappearance,
something like that.
I think it's natural.

Positive

Father hominid, construction worker,
it's like Canada out here.
You still go out of your way.

Service

It's definitely a one-way street.
The other departments are the clients.
There shouldn't be much expectation
other than a donut every once in a while.
They are under no obligation.

Involvement

I know you think it's idiotic.
(It means everything these days!)
It is characterized with words that
provoke emergency response thinking.
Do you stick your nose in
and obstruct firefighters?
That's the way I feel about all this.
Later, there might be discussions about
decapitations and public executions,
I would just get in the way there too.

Home Taking

It's one of those things
where you know it's going on,
it has an almost naturalness to it.
Cause and effect, supply and demand—
a branch of the human anatomy is failing,
a family is being thrown out of their house.

I don't get that emotional about it.
I'm glad I was on this side of the taking though.
I wonder about the taker.

Not Quite Taken

The other boys are playing.
Bright sunshine after rain
steaming up the parking lot
near the back door of the music studio
where you both spent the night.
So natural and so beautiful.
You remember what day of the week it is.
You are going to the Corner Inn
for steak and eggs.

Fed Up

I don't think I can keep up
this bullshit storm much longer—
some kind of twenty-person acrobatic team
with hula hoops.
The eye surveys pockets of the performance,
and is amazed at the precision and interaction of it.
This convinces the experiencer of reality
to allow in what must be true—
there is something even more perfect
than what is being perceived.
This opens up the possibility of transcendence.

Oblivious

If things continue along these lines,

and I start to repeat myself,
I guess I don't mind you telling me,
but I feel terrible about it enough already.
(It isn't happening; never mind.)

Performance Ark

"That was different."
A reasonable assumption is
that there is
a subliminal storage of behaviors—
style, affect—surface things.
But is this part of the mind receptive to
certain patterns only?
The rest completely forgotten?
Is there a final filter for something (maybe) worthwhile?
Or are they all in there—
and the one socially "appropriate" released?

Chronology

That movie with the aliens with the bulbous heads,
the ones that injected the teenagers with alcohol
and had syringes for claws—
I thought they were claws—
for years.
Line leaders for going salt water fishing at Alki,
and I imagined fish hooks for fingernails,
and catching footballs,
for years.

Unwitting Actor

One thing I am pretty sure of,
I am walking a fine line with these delusions.
I am trying to add some dimension to everyone now.
I am interpreting new scenarios,
with the added disassociation of me in the drama.
It's not real. It's delusions having delusions
and me.

Post It

I understand anxiety—
the shaking, the heart swarm, the truth.
I am exploring it to possibly make it explainable
to the scientific community.

Monolith

Fluid part of air rumbling overhead,
we understand way more sounds
than anything else in the universe.
Boom?
Dictionary, checkmate.

Translate

I highlight the ideal
and obscure the real,
you're the art.
No spark in empty clay,
death is always plain.

Masked Images

It is not good. The exterior is still up.
God is still here. Not in the right mindset?
My attention is absorbed. I am creeping up on it.
Paw, paw, paw.
A vital, natural, pouncing thought, I see it,
walls being sealed around me, I am more isolated.

Pseudo Man

I think I've evolved.
The thought patterns they've installed
have produced the reason to think in
extraterrestrial ways.
Which is a problem,
because human brain tissue
is hard for even them to understand.

Sting

Projecting a weakness of mine upon all of you:
I can no longer recognize bad intentions,
and I rely too much on rumor
and the interpretation of innuendo
to make up for that weakness.
I think almost everyone has this disability.
Petty prejudices, mostly.
I still get taken advantage of a lot.
That's usually the bad intention towards me.
It's not so much the twenty bucks,
what really hurts about it is the lack of respect.
That is why I still refer to information
that is usually so wrong.
For those given an overabundance of respect,

even grudgingly, they must feel it as malice.
God help you if you're Jang Song Thaek.

Stinger

Remove all hatred. Go on.
The other is still the other
no matter how transparent.
Moving forward—
no intimate detail shared,
no opinion in war,
complete loyalty in peace.
(It will still go on underneath all of that.)

Overalls

I wander about among people.
You can't expect me to be the same.
I want to be everyone else.
You don't have to look.

Spiral

It is not happening.
That word *confidence* Eric used
was only an attempt at a little humor.
The tinge of insult that was felt was all that it was.
No objective reality motivated that subjective response.
Constantly aware,
trips planned,
routines changed,
shirts ironed,
that is not the way to live.

The innerness of it is hard to describe.
It always takes on world views,
and always is personally involved.
It has that in common with virtue.
A black-and-white judgment
would have to go along with it.
That's where I lose it.
I will keep it under observation.
Confidence…

Watch Me

Getting away from danger,
that is going to be my mantra.
I know how to behave,
that will be too.
Wednesday informs Thursday,
I will become the conductor of reality,
a boxer in a defensive pose,
Dorian Gray,
all these things in a calm walk.

Personality Prison

I do not have to follow through on things.
If nature and behavior force me
to act a certain way today,
that does not mean I should act
that way tomorrow.
Use this knowledge responsibly.

Clickety Clack

I am lonely.
Pics uploaded.
I am settled, so naturally adventurous:
"However it has happened, I find myself bohemian.
As far away from New Age as one can get,
but still stealing the garbage they peddle—
making it up better, making it true.
I sell a lot of them."

Met with Shrugged Shoulders

Slide down from papa now.
You are competition.
This isn't working.

Fiction Formula

The impossible doesn't ever occur.
And I am in opposition to the dream.
These two keep it flowing—
pressure from both sides.
I am not very good.
This dawns on me later.

Necktie

Produced out of nowhere,
and applied to one's advantage,
that is all that that is.
I've never heard voices, or seen anything—
except this…
A woman was lying flat on the grass
wearing an almost old fashioned

plaid petticoat, sensible handbag,
and her hands were clasped at her waist.
She was just lying there.
Feet pointed straight at me.
Picture Hazel dressed like Mary Poppins.
When I was nine, I was in the Patrols.
We were crossing guards.
We helped control two busy intersections.
One was right on the corner of the school,
the other was a good two blocks away—
completely out of sight of the school.
Almost everyone walked to school,
most without their moms.
I think there were five postings a day
to catch the kids coming and going—
the late birds, the early birds,
and the kindergartners.
The kindergartners got off around lunch.
The east side of the isolated intersection
had two non-houses.
They were across the busy street from each other.
The corner nearer the school,
the corner where I was supposed
to wait for the kindergartners,
had a dark gray, brown nothing there—
a two-story box.
It did have an inviting backyard; it looked like
it could be a good shortcut
if you were turning east on 56th.
But there was no outlet.
Just a solid wooden fence,
This is where I saw the woman.

I can't imagine what this building
was used for originally,
let alone in 1974.
I'm guessing for a very 1973 reason.
I never saw anyone (else) there.
The building did have an unobstructed view
of Sandpoint Naval Air Station though.
Its sister across the street had "Sisters"
hand painted on one of its store front windows.
This window was frequently broken.
I heard the word lesbian for the first time.
I also heard about witches.
This building looked like it actually used to be a house.
It was a lighter shade of brown-gray.
This lot had a similarly inviting potential shortcut.
Theirs was fenced off, though, by a chain-link fence.
And it was made even more impenetrable
by what looked to be an attempt at a corn patch.
I never remember that ever being green.
I never remember seeing anyone there either.
The front windows by the front door
were always darkly curtained.
From the roof, it also had a clear view of Sandpoint.

Pine Box

Addiction is only endurable when it is admitted so.
A relapse almost always makes the former addict the star,
a person with a master plan, someone in control.
The most fragile of conditions and such confidence!

Observer

Camping gear is melancholy.
A relapse—
"La la la la, sweet Jane."
His glassy stare of death—
the orange streaks,
ourselves reflecting on his corpse.

Pardon Me

Insight starts seeking out people to write to here.
It won't be the *mind your own business* type stuff,
it will just be me imagining I'm speaking
to whom I imagine you must be.
I find much success when I'm violated—
it will be something you will want to hear.

How We Must Relate

Force is the word that comes to mind.
A super magnet!
Drive? That only had the "d" and "r" going for it.
A super machine!
It has to be bigger than what you think.

My Wishing Well

Echo is a severe judgment on humanity.
It is gone.
Only beautiful to the vainly expectant.
No longer able to spellbind.
That is how it is.
It must be dealt with.
Prostrate yourself to that fact.

Nibiru

To accomplish the natural face (manners),
my philosophy compels me
to accept the superiority of the forces of my ego.
I really do think I'm better than everyone else—
that person's religion is crazy,
that person is a clown,
that person is politically stupid.
Maybe only to counteract my servile condition,
but I have become open to those truths.

Toxic

Testosterone pollutes the blood a little bit—
am I hearing an implied permission to proceed?
Almost all martyrs are considered very stupid people.
Variation in degree, but all in the pile at Jonestown.
Going because others have gone,
and for the dumbest of reasons.
*Wills bent by constant observation
and conformity—of course they will.*

Poem Bot

I wake up and find the surgical wounds.
Their endoscopy technology is wonderful.
Just about every vascular pathway too.
I feel so violated.
But the neurological agents—
that come before, and come after,
they make me feel so good.
And they give me a raging erection too.

They're getting all the good stuff, guys.
This protein bag is producing desired results.

Lover

"It can't just be what he says," meaning himself,
I imagine him saying.

Observations and Topic Changes

Sometimes I interrupt. I'm sorry. I'm old.
If I think of something appropriate
while somebody is still talking,
I have to concentrate really hard not to forget it.
Maybe miss things, important things.
It's like a double loss—
high hopes and a "I just said that."

Cell

I lie there thinking things over.
Twentieth century history,
it all ends in the middle,
and it ends with an atomic bomb.
That is the period.
Then I just forget the rest of it,
everything else that led up to it,
from both ways.
I lose the whole train of thought,
and along with that, the climax.
I just see the explosion and no point.

Draining

Is that it, sapping?
Is that where you get your strength?
Exposing a vein and agonizing?
That is your deeper existence?
It's not at all charming in real life,
it's all monster.

Provincial

I feel I bring out the agent provocateur in some people,
and that's here in my own hometown.
You would think I would have the freedom
to be a jerk in my own hometown.
I think, where you're suggesting, Paris,
that would be the least of my worries.
Young males would certainly harm me physically.
I would pretty much be considered less than
by almost everyone; and be treated with
open hostility on a way-too-often basis.
If one-tenth of what I'm saying is true,
I shouldn't have to go on.
But I'm being mild.
I would have to disavow
almost everything that is American,
and be convincing in my rage.
I ask the immigrant here:
Would that be tolerable for one second?

Ogopogo

This is the fish you've flopped onto your boat.
It smells a bit and breathes in water.
It is different from you.

Frolic

Juan, Stan, I'm 53.
I am going to retire in nine years.
I seem an unwise investment.
For only a minimal return
(a few years of a polished office professional),
you will be giving up years of solid productivity.
I think I'm best suited entering required information
in data fields, with little knowledge
of the ultimate purpose of it all.

Fish Bowl

I have a riddle for you:
Where does a plane go before it crashes?
Down.
The cold blood has to circulate out,
the new, in.
The monster must be fed.
"Hey buddy how's it going?"
(I gave him the finger.)
I wonder if I will look like my poster.
Buying some gas, "Cheese!"
Dreadlocks! Dude, you're going to be famous.

Man, What an Ego

The sod tries to face off that which is bigger,
and coughs and fails,
every time.
The helmet will not have it.
Best to give it obsequience.

Don't Move

Visualize the pod.
I am of the pod,
I am in the pod.
Invade the Earth.
Run over Kevin McCarthy.
Kill him.
Whisper, whisper, whisper.

Ease

Fluorescence, brilliance, opulence,
architectural angles, attendants—
pour something into me.
No, it has to be a nothing.
That is the only way.
The craftsmanship, style, cleanliness—nope.
Respond, navigate, and leave the door unlocked.

Wednesday

I just came from space.
My exterior is a biosynthetic.
That is all I know.
But that seems to mean everything.
The breathing in *2001* is very claustrophobic.

Dad

The head and the eyes oriented on the mouth.
Nowhere near the same level.
Peck, peck, peck.
Violently broken through, eventually.

But for now, the teeth and gums,
they're nice too.
O God, I'm learning things!

Flair

An office building after business hours—
can I say that is where I fell asleep?
Is that too obscure?
I cut my little finger punching down deli trash
to tie a knot.
Bled for days.
Threw my back out the first time,
trying to fish out a card that fell behind a desk.
Hurt for a month.
I hate to be cryptic.

Mental Echoing

Mathematically hypnotic when done on purpose.
In accidental nature, informative in a Taoist sense.
It's the opening scenes of *Saturday Night Fever*
and *Being There*.

Blood Brain Barrier

Watchers, guardians, morning stars—prehistoric.
No word for ruthless, no word for normal,
lots of victims.
I understand the attraction.
Righteousness won't take me back; it takes me
further away.

Displacement

The chorus sings in unison.
It is singular and the star.
It can handle the big roles.
It's also artificial, immortal, and loud.
I miss a lot of the meaning.
I heard a doctor talk about learning strategies
for medical students once.
His advice was general when it came to retention—
learning should feel hard.
I think the Athenians scratched their beards too.

Sound

Scrolling up to the source,
capillaries circuitous,
there is osmosis going on,
cellular respiration.
Words are cells.
I acknowledge the binary nature of it,
binary like logic and most star systems—
mass, calculations, equal signs, orbits,
no matter how much weight you put upon them,
the things other than words are there too.

Lines

More piano jazz music now
for my free hour.
Imagine a tree frog's sticky hands
crawling all over a barky tree.
The analogy works both ways.

Arts and Entertainment

Makes no difference in a cosmic sense.
So important to us—alone.
SETI?
I guess the fact is we're in a universal jar.
We hope the animals smile and cry.

Pep Talk

Let's say there is a half a billion
English speaking people left in the world.
Those aren't human beings,
they're potential customers!

DSM-5

All of everything can be acute or chronic,
and with degrees of severity.
Saying I'm in there doesn't say much.
The paranoid in Shanghai
missed being enslaved and drowned.

Quarter

My six-foot shadow cast at sunset,
sorry, I was startled.
Conscience?
The freak was I thought you were my brother.
Didn't want him to know about the weed.
Drama, comedy—the accidental becomes logical.
It's like the final vote after a contentious penultimate,
the making it unanimous.
The willful changing of the vote, however disingenuous,

activates something central in the mind.
I am putting you in the credits, conscience.

First Cyber Attack

This thought carries a lot freight:
This would be a perfect time to die,
or the *most ironic*, or *saddest*.
Drama does not exist in the natural universe.
Only in our minds.
If we have to debate that, stop reading.
You can't even lay that one on God.
But that's just my opinion.
I have an idea about who is behind this.
Conscience wants me to budge.
Not to admit guilt,
but to acquiesce to its authority.
The authority is not acquiesced to.

Martial Arts Attack

Destroyed by themselves just doesn't have
the same memorable quality as brimstone.
And suicide is not the same thing.
Conscience is atrophied here leading up to it.
I do not want a weakened conscience
just because it's stupid and illogical.
Such an end is slow and violent.
It touches our sensibilities to the point where
we have to write a story about it.
We live in an advanced society, fiction is okay.
I see the conscience grabbing some ego here too.
Maybe, just maybe, perceiving the lack of

itself in the morality tale (or in reality),
it borrows for the drama the ego.
I think that affects the recounting of history.

Time Out

As the rent went up into the double digits,
I was already well into mine.
And the final number isn't even that.
You have the goddamn
water, sewer, and trash fee, too.
So it's always some
fucking number that ends in cents.

Settlement

Motor neurons manipulate the environment.
Perception—wavelengths on the rebound.
There is projection, too, from the inside.
And the six-foot confrontation,
I give you one-quarter.

To Big Brother

The tactless and careless
don't give a shit if they offend.
So confrontation is pointless.
It will not reduce my output.
Forward through time—
destroying like Columbus
with SafeSearch on, and hidden.

Stay with Cleopatra

We have money and are combining.
Putting together a team.
We are normal citizens and are correct.
We are shooting for full voluntary participation.
Another group like us is leaving.
We are moving in.

Ted Baxter

The feeling is not shared. Doesn't that bother you?
If that kind of intrusiveness is considered normal,
then I truly do not belong here.
You really envision a fully integrated community of workers,
who all have genuine affection for one another?
Any level-headed person analyzing that thought
would say that it is very delusional.

Blare

More cries from mortal to mortal.
I bet the animals see it.
Unweaned, loud sucklings.
I know the angels do.
Geez.
Anyway, that's the way I see it.

Cover-Up

Something that is true and obscured on purpose.
(As long as I'm in here, I'll have a look around.)
I've had it together for so long,
I've become a mark for my own con.
There isn't anything too wrong with that.

It can be a beautiful thing actually.
That's the way my totality is expressed, though,
all the time.

Gremlin

The ego wants to do more.
It speaks its sense with equal force up against
the objectively perceived.
It can be punk rock, the news, drama—
"Do you like that? Abracadabra."
I listen.

Maxim #6

Unique is a pro wrestling punch in the face.
Genuine is a real punch in the face

Subroutine #1

Cynical doesn't even come close.
It reaches the point of paranoia at times.
That's how not close.
There is so much that I've experienced over the years
that shows how uninformed this way of thinking is,
that one would think that I would have learned to ignore it,
and certainly not to validate it.
But I haven't and do sometimes.
The fact that I would be looked down upon
by snotty, insecure know-it-alls
at almost every lunch or get together
is never questioned.
It causes narratives to be formed too.

And even when some little part of that drama
is disproved outright,
as when my conservative Christian
back story of Mabel was shredded
by her absolute admitted Marxism,
it's still true, it survives that.
Just the Red Brigade is involved
in whatever 'it' is.
It doesn't affect the way I treat people, much.
It is total self-judgment—I am in over my head.
The purpose of it is self-protection.

In Bones

I am poisoned. If it had a taste,
it would be aftershave.
It would also be those shoes with toes,
and soundtracks,
and Captain Stubing.
I am not going to Puerto Vallarta,
but almost everyone else is.
It is a migration.
No one in their right mind can stop it.
Splash.

Condensed Population

The runner trapped, still runs.
Emptiness and virtuosity,
and living as freely as any person in history,
not really noticed.

Inevitable Presence

I'm having a lot of endings lately.
That poor fellow in Dystopia there.
And don't forget the Titanic before that.

Amblyopia

You forgot most interesting and best looking.
No, I saw that smile on your face.
And you were seriously blushing.
You were all like, "Damn, he's really into me."
Your face was almost breaking.
You were not just a form.
The ridiculousness of it surpassed that.
The symbiotic, escalating, critical massing of it—
just kept getting more intense, right?

Antibodies

Any glimpse of it is immediately
recognized as being foreign
and cloture is passed.

Giza

So similar, so exact,
in every member—
a species. How awful.
Locked in. Hatched out.
It's like the reliefs
of gods with bird's heads.
Being human is so much cooler—
even if you are an oppressor of thousands.

An Ibis? I'll be the Sphinx. Give me the body.

Scanner

Look at each face.
"Welcome."
"Tickets."
"This way."
Not a jersey.
A sensible windbreaker.
Orange.
Very slender.
"One moment."
Extra scrutiny.
She went to the luxury suite elevators.

Nature

When you put this flower
underneath your chin,
it shines yellow if you like butter.
"Everyone knows that, stupid!"
(Learn new things.)

Miles Off

Paper instead of flesh,
this state of mind expressed.
Keeping it for real, it's fiction.
A screened door—
I still have respect for you, dirty things,
just the air, if you don't mind.
The flesh will not be ignored, be careful.

Progress

Tall stone, granite, carved,
geometry, astronomy, pyramids—
modern.
The functioning hovels
within eccentric streets,
shortcuts, the temple, sheep,
goats, and grain—more beautiful.

Drugged

I am not alone.
I am not. That is an illusion.
These people are here.
"Toss the supplies, first."
See? I heard that,
That car horn a million miles away—
I heard that too.
Someone knows, they will put an end to this.
I am not claustrophobic.
I will be calm when I'm untied and unwrapped.
I probably shouldn't be awake.
My radar picked up the urgency
of the situation and metabolized me awake.
I'm probably paralyzed. I can't move at all.
All resources have been redirected
to the command center to strategize
my way out of this.
God?
Oh! So cold! Right through the plastic too.
I barely felt the gravity going down.
Water in my lungs.

First principles.

Review

It may seem surprising,
but gut sharing criticism is not my thing.
That is science, the arts, business, politics—
sophistication.
Guess what?

Personnel Matter

I am the pebble. The ocean is dropped on me.
Even smaller now. Hard to move.
Think on the stars. They do not exist.
Categorize space. Join me down here.
I await. You cannot.

Progress Note

Albert has once again harvested
the same construct.
The restraints have been removed.
Subject is notable for having total avoidance
of wrists and legs.
Will not look at them.
Starting to doubt the diagnosis.

Levels

You said you lost a little respect for me
because of the way I'm dressed.
You could have said many other things of me

along the same line.
I know I'm fine.
I don't need your approval.
(You lost a little of my initial respect too.)
But now you've gone too far,
extrapolating that prejudice into some kind of
objectively observed reality
that can be backed up with hard data.
I decline your business, sorry.

Ghostbuster

The sprightly nurse ravishes her mind.
The only thing left.
She's here
in my apartment that I share with my brother.
She flits about dropping treasures
for her thoughtless habitants.
And spinning around laughing.
Emptiness and emptiness,
at least it's something.
It's everything.
That fine hotel soap in its original package,
c. 1900,
just getting wet in the corner.
Each of us thinking the other had left it there,
not even bothering to unwrap it.
"There is only one kind of person
that should be allowed to use this soap,
it is a lover on vacation in Paris.
No one else."
I ask in real time (because I actually did hear that):

Why did you leave that buffalo-shaped bar, then?
So here is New York State, and Niagara Falls,
American animals, and 1950?
I will be that for you, my dear, since it is incorporeal.
I will hang out with you in the kitchenette.
Share a glass or two from the little stocked bar.
And we'll drink ourselves onto the linoleum floor.
The smell of sperm drifting in from the bedroom
and the cigarette smoke clogging your pores
are making you visible and raw—
O god! Your hips!

Borrower

Head in the clouds—literally;
because there is no other legitimate
way of expressing it.
Delusion has a cloudy aspect to it, agreed,
but that word is way too noisy.
If inspired didn't have such a possessive quality,
it would do.

Doctor Gray

My head is not thinking clearly on this.
I am susceptible to having my irrational fears, sorry.
I am only appreciated for my body.
I am always questioned, never befriended.
Mortal alien, nice see you again.

Inoculation

You see, almost everyone around here

figured out the world at fifteen.
Rule one, look out for yourself.
People don't care about you.
You're tolerated as long as you're distant.
And everyone who tries to be friends with you
actually does wants to be friends with you.
Rule two, friends.

Danger!

My mind says to kill.
Society says otherwise.
I almost want to die, so bad the other can be.
God, these things equal out on each other.
Instinct is free to act, finally!

Subtle

So crafty in humans,
you could almost say sly.
And cold-blooded too.
I will defeat my enemy
outside of the law.

Akimbo

Ease, thin bodies in opposition.
The wolf inside will always sense danger.
That's just where humanity is right now.
You are not wrong to realize that.
Don't feel guilty.
It's too easy for truth like that to descend into angst
when guilt is added to it.

Left Bank

Do I feel a sense of waste?
The smells not experienced?
Background, depth, foreground, colors?
Soul searching conversation, political debate, performing?
Echoes and no echoes?
I guess a little. Everybody else is doing it.
I am pretty comfortable the way I am though.
And I'm doing it pretty well.

A Real Guy

Room,
same floor forever,
school paper,
Writers Guild,
radio stations,
advertising,
painting,
such good friends,
drinking.
Old and sore,
diseased,
the worst of everything,
addicted,
war on opioids.

A Lady

Prank stare,
blame the victim,
imagine a plague,

sit in judgment,
and vow to be more violent in the future.
Cold,
standing over your cowed victims,
proud of your brutality—
and direct threats for more!

A Wasp

Blow,
legs around,
old fashioned,
swallow,
tongue,
fantasy,
mature,
rut.

A Black Coat

I walk innocent out of abject oppression.
And invent innocence after that.
I am not like others.
I'm justified in heaven. I am of the cloth,
tailored animism.
Enjoying a good trope and a brioche this morning.

A Doctor on a Bike

Plastic as in artificial,
only bendable as the group turns.

Me

Imagine 1960s data sound effects
on a 1970s TV show—
The Six Million Dollar Man,
and an android breaking down
in varying intensities of close-up—
camera 25 degrees askew.

A Graybeard

Don't be a Socrates; let us have our larks.
Imitating him has never worked in history.
He's always had the luxury
of being a million years dead.
He's beyond cross-examination himself.

Error

Things close to other things,
not parasites or suckerfish,
just things close to other things.
Getting away because people are bad,
and getting away because I am bad.

Aimed

No power (of course), dusty, moldy, unlived in.
Forensics could tell I've walked through,
no one else could.
Upstairs, it's exactly like a hundred thousand others.
Cannot tell that this is only half the basement.
Look at all the space those oxygen tanks take up!
Only the false broadcasts on the ham.
Everything else guessed at.

I never feel the vibrations anymore.
Brutal oppression over!
Wild celebrations in the streets!
I wonder how many coups there've really been.
Probably none.
Footsteps! Footsteps! Footsteps!
Only one—
booming sledgehammer, kitchen floor—
only one.
I am mapped out, pinpointed.
Filamentous light banging through the ceiling.
I am here, too, waiting for a target.
Now along my flank after a few footfalls
down the stairs,
you're hammering on my poor wall.
Crashing, raining in more debris on my head.

Incessant Ionic Dance

The odd rolls down, collecting,
sometimes replacing, but mostly collecting
more numbers.
I am permanently stuck in a preliminary program,
and I am abandoned.

Sumerian Proverb

When you get close to their yards,
dogs bark their brains out.

Magic

It is only limited in its personal aspect.

It is general.
There are organizations that no matter what
kind of face they may put forward,
they will not be liked or trusted.
I'm sure an example is easily imagined.
I was not only very good at my job,
I was probably one of the best ever.
It is not my personality to be the center
of physical attention. I had to reach past that
into things like logic, recognition, culture,
and general knowledge to achieve a personality
that best approximated my somewhat unusual one.
Being friendly and fake does not work.
That is a brainwashed.
I worked at the desk, not some schism.
And I am terrible actor!
I was at the desk.
Maybe some of you are feeling a bit pressed.
I felt it back then.
I put my name out there.
Maybe be a little less public.
And make a lot more money too!
I saw one "or equivalent experience"
and decided to apply. It felt good.
Applied to seven clinics in all
to be their front desk representative.
Me.
Tailored my resume so there would be no doubt
as to who was applying for their position—
one of the best in the world.
I realized I would have to learn some things,
technical things. Check that—

I would have had to learn a lot.
But whatever portion customer service
is assigned in the metrics of this organization,
I'd have to have the highest score in that—ever.
Like I said, seven clinics.
Within a few weeks, "considered, not selected"
began appearing in my application status windows.
Eventually, four out of seven.
The last one (because two never did respond) had
someone arrange to speak with me the next day
for a phone interview. It was a ten minute
conversation that was followed thirty minutes
later with a "considered, not selected" message.
Now I am unemployed and isolated—
and furniture and a television set is all I have.
Why must it be so opposite!
Loved, envied, desired—and hated.
I turn on the set.
Personal care, sexual characteristics,
intelligence—next channel, the first thirty minutes
of Invasion of the Body Snatchers, 1978.
Hmm…
A discussion show, an anecdote,
a Japanese woman's passive aggression—
displeased with her mother-in-law,
she misarranges the flowers.

To India

I don't know if you played it over there,
but over here, we actually played musical chairs
at school sponsored events.

Can you imagine?

Back Float

There is just rudimentary reasoning
when it comes to things like traffic flow.
It's just a lot of cars going this way and that.
Eventually, the drawing of an inference—
a nearby highway and a time of day.
It doesn't really go much further than that.
Wrong turns in reality? Yeah.

Didn't Even Wake Me Up

Cathartic, kaleidoscopic, primal, sublime,
five days' growth of beard, a bag of mosquitos,
buried up to my chin, meat hooks.

In Crayon

Here is how it doesn't work:
Giving a gift to appease anger,
expecting good for good.
Like a lot of things,
it does work a little in the beginning.
It never really feels right though.
And it eventually implodes.
When this disappoints enough times,
some of us quit bothering with gods
or injured people anymore, and just imagine
deficits that need to be filled in other individuals.
Please forgive me is replaced by *please like me*.
A trick to really be wary of is absorbing

that *wanting* to mean as Merriam-Webster puts it,
"not being up to standards or expectations".
When that happens,
the magic has completely turned on its attempted user.

www.ingramcontent.com/pod-product-compliance
Lightning Source LLC
Chambersburg PA
CBHW060501080526
44584CB00015B/1505